CW00515104

How to Remov Devices from Your Amazon Account: AND Add New Device to Your Amazon Account: Picture Guide

© 2017 Christabel Mattox

due to the information contained herein be it direct or indirect.

The information offered here is for the purposes of information only and is universal as such. The information presented here is without any form of contract or guarantee or indemnity whether with the reader or any third party.

HOW TO REMOVE KINDLE DEVICE FROM AMAZON ACCOUNT

Once you have used kindle devices for a period of time, you would have observed how easy for your old devices to pile up on your list. However, you can decide to make it easier by removing your old kindle devices. The reason for this is simple. Most of the times, you may change your device. Although they have been changed, your old device will still remain in your kindle. You will have your android/iPhone or iPad device on your amazon account. Amazon has provided an avenue for managing your devices and your ebooks.

We will give you a step by step tutorial guide on how to manage your kindle account with the latest guide.

Log into your amazon account by providing your email and your password.

Hover your mouse over your account. A drop down menu appears.

Click on your content and your devices.

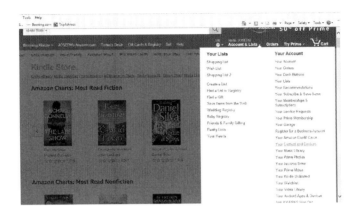

Next, the screen below displays.

Choose the device as shown in the pictorial guide below.

Under this tab, all the kindle devices that have been registered on your account both kindle apps, kindles devices, or cloud will all be shown under this tab. Each of the device has email address attached to it. From the picture above, we have just three devices.

However, it can be more complicated if the devices are up to seven or eight in the number. The devices all have email addresses attached to them for the purposes of sending other documents such as ebooks, pdf, and image files.

If you want to organise these devices, the first step that you have to take is to rename them for easy identification. The Kindle apps on your iPhone, tablet, and computer do not have this capacity. The only option is to use amazon website.

To organise your device, click on either of the devices by selecting the action button on the left hand cover. You will see three dots on it.

Then click on the edit button.

Remove Old Kindle & Add New Kindle

Type the name of the device and click on save.

Edit Device Information ✕

You can tell your devices apart by giving each one a unique name.

Device Name: [H's Android Samnsur ✕ |]

Cancel   Save

You will get a successful notification.

After renaming the ones that you know that you need, then you may have to delete those ones that are no longer needed. You have to be sure that it is a device that you don't need. You can remove it from your kindle account. The simplest way to do is as follows.

Select the device that you know you don't want anymore and click on deregister.

The moment you click on deregister, you will get confirmation page telling you that once you deregister, the app will no longer be available on your device. Select deregister.

Deregister this device ✕

Your Device will be deregistered from your Amazon account. This will remove all content from the device and many features will not work. Items you purchased from an Amazon store will remain available in the Cloud and can be downloaded again. After deregistering, you can register your Device to another Amazon account. Are you sure you want to deregister?

Cancel | Deregister

After doing that, it becomes easy for you to know which device that you will purchase your books to from the kindle store. If for instance, I want to buy an ebook, and I will click on the buy now with 1 click, under the "deliver to," I will be presented with a lot of options. From our tutorial above, I will see Joseph's Kindle cloud and Joseph's Android Samsung 8. I will just send it to the appropriate device.

HOW TO ADD NEW KINDLE DEVICE TO YOUR AMAZON ACCOUNT.

The procedure that I have outlined is beautiful. But after removing the old devices, you may want to a new device to your kindle. The old device is gone, and a new device should be added. I will show you how to do that in 2 Minutes

First, I assumed you already have an existing amazon kindle. If you don't, then you have to create an account.

Choose your language. If you are English, then select one or UK English. I selected US English.

Deutsch

English (United Kingdom)

English (United States)

Español

Français

Italiano

日本語

Português (Brasil)

简体中文

Next Connect to a WIFI. For the purposes of this registration, make sure that you have a stable connection.

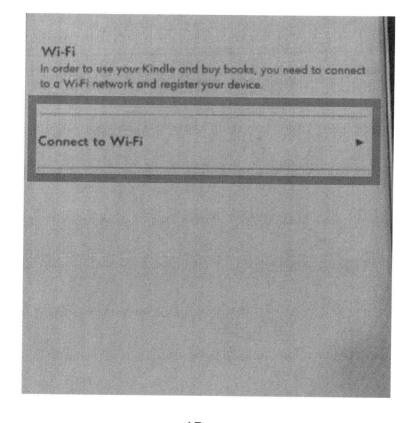

Then   choose   your   WIFI.

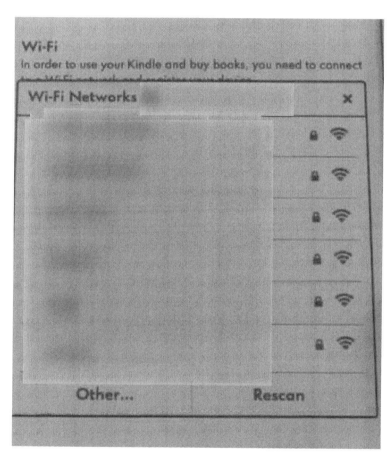

Remove Old Kindle & Add New Kindle

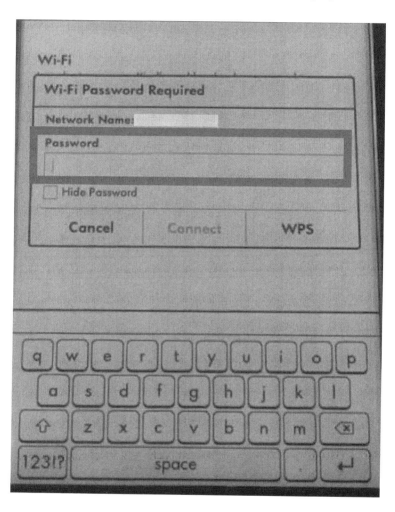

Enter your WIFI Password as shown in the screen above.

It will connect to Amazon and show you the next step that you should take.

Connecting to Amazon...

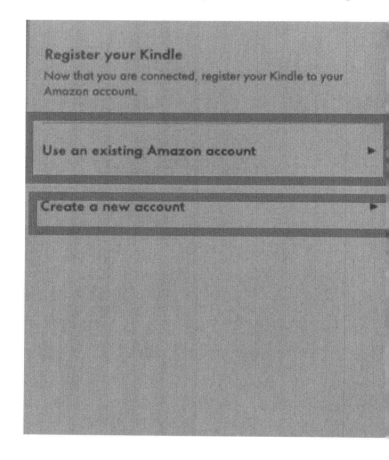

At this stage, select existing Amazon Account if you have an amazon account or create a new account if you don't have one.

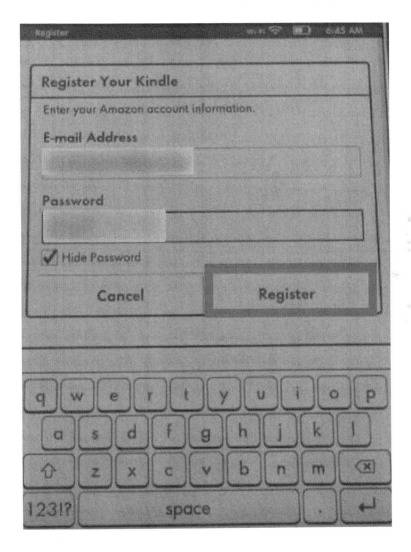

Next, choose register when you have entered your amazon password and email address.

Confirming your registration...

It will register your account.

I will show you through another book of mine how to transfer all of your books to your new kindle. I mean everything with Pdf documents and files downloaded from third party sites, just look at this book. No stress in 20 minutes maximum you are done.

Amazon.com: How to Transfer Books from Old Kindle to New Kindle: A 10 Minutes Picture Guide for All IPad, IPhone, Kindle Paperwhite, Touch, Nook, Kindle Oasis,

Kindle ... Kindle Voyage, Kindle HD Fire,

etc. eBook: Christabel Mattox: Kindle Store

OTHER BOOKS BY THE

SAME AUTHOR

HOW TO DELETE BOOKS OFF YOUR KINDLE: A Complete Step by Step Picture Guide on How to Delete Books From All Kindle Devices Plus Paperwhite, HD Fire, iPad,iPhone, etc., in 2 Minutes, 2017 Latest Guide

The scond Edition of my Book, How to Delete books off your Kindle is out. It has three Bonuses inside. 1 Audio File, and two Bonuses: Kindle Tips and Tricks, and how to Detete Books on Kindle Elnk 5 way Controller. Check it out.

HOW TO DELETE BOOKS FROM YOUR

KINDLE: Plus Tips & Tricks Every KIndle

31

Owner Must Know (2nd Edition) eBook:

Christabel Mattox

4 in 1 Kindle: A Picture Guide on How to Cancel Kindle Unlimited Subscription in 2 minutes, Remove Kindle Device from Amazon Account, Cancel Amazon 1-Click Order and Get Your Money Refunded in Quickly, etc

Kodi: The Complete Beginners Guide to

Setup Kodi 17.3

Installing Kodi 17.3 Krypton On Amazon
Firestick From Beginner To Pro: Complete
Step by Step Picture Guide on How to Setup
and Install Kodi 17.3 Krypton on Fire stick

Amazon.com: AMAZON ALEXA & AMAZON ECHO FROM BEGINNER TO PRO: Complete Step by Step Guide on How to install and Setup

Other books by the same Author

Installing Kodi 17.3 Krypton On Amazon
Firestick From Beginner To Pro: Complete

Step by Step Picture Guide on How to Setup

and Install Kodi 17.3 Krypton on Fire stick

Amazon.com: AMAZON ALEXA &
AMAZON ECHO FROM BEGINNER TO
PRO: Complete Step by Step Guide on How
to install and Setup

Kodi: The Complete Beginners Guide to

Setup Kodi 17.3

Christabel Mattox

Christabel Mattox

Printed in Great Britain
by Amazon